TOLSTOY'S
ANNA KARENINA
Quotes

Adult Coloring Book for Literature Lovers

Source
All quotes were collected from Project Gutenberg's e-book of *Anna Karenina*, by Leo Tolstoy, translated by Constance Garnett. This translation of *Anna Karenina* is part of the public domain and available to read for free at www.gutenberg.org.

SWEET PEA LILY

THIS BOOK
BELONGS TO

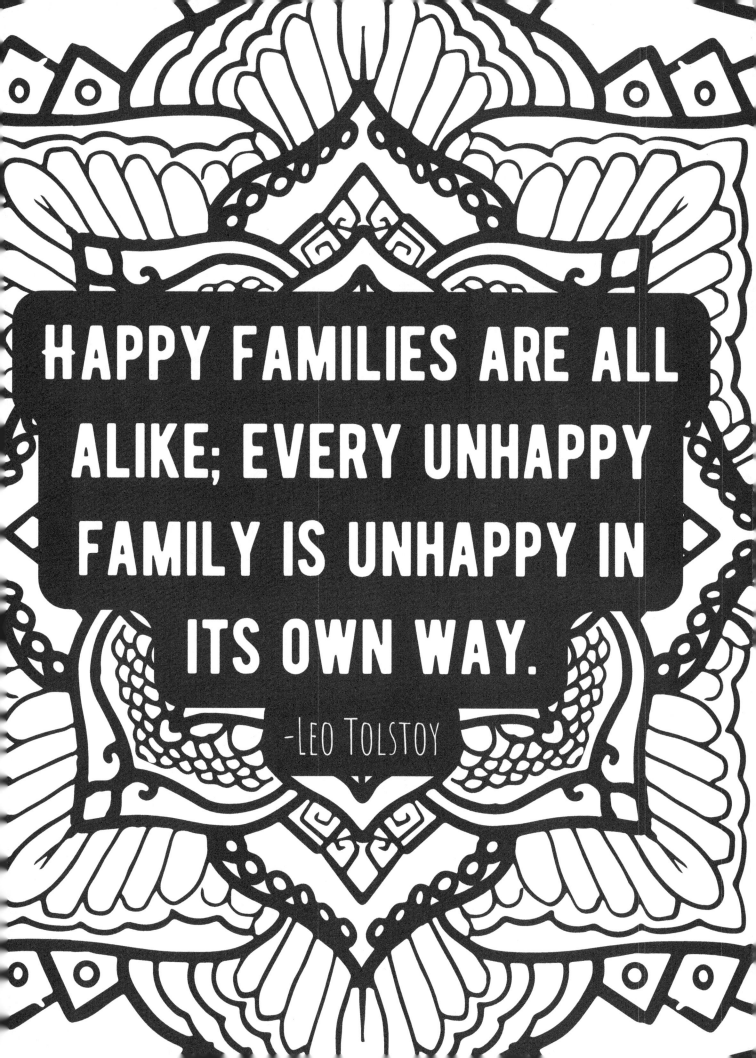

HAPPY FAMILIES ARE ALL ALIKE; EVERY UNHAPPY FAMILY IS UNHAPPY IN ITS OWN WAY.

-LEO TOLSTOY

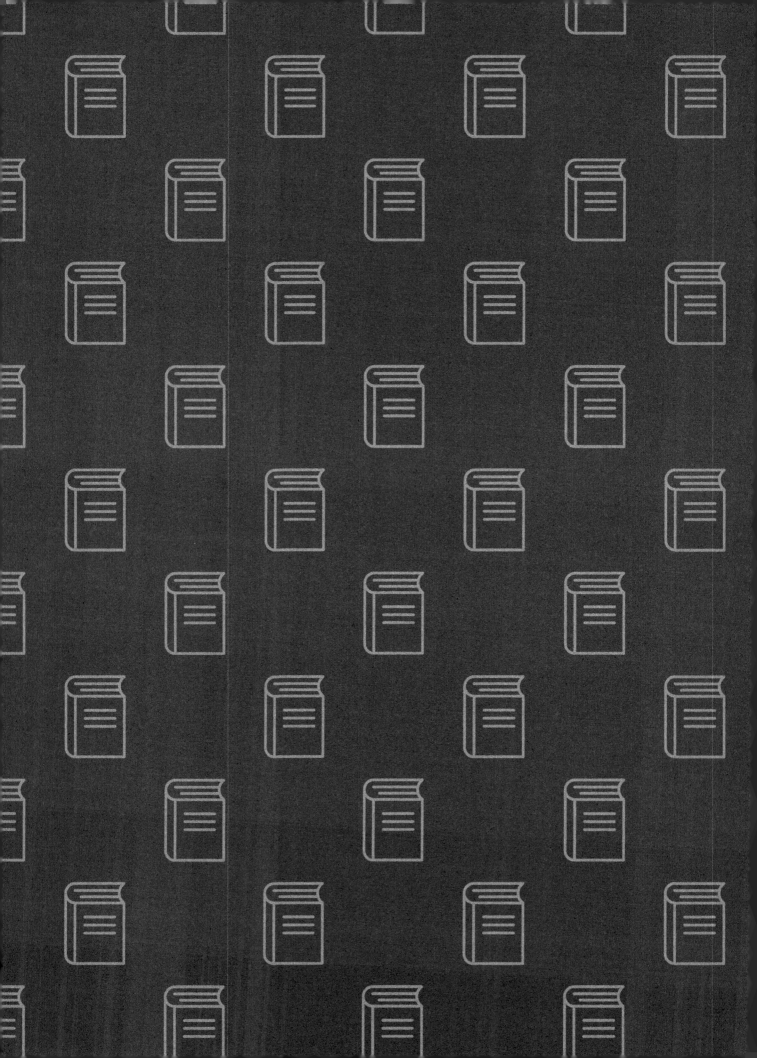

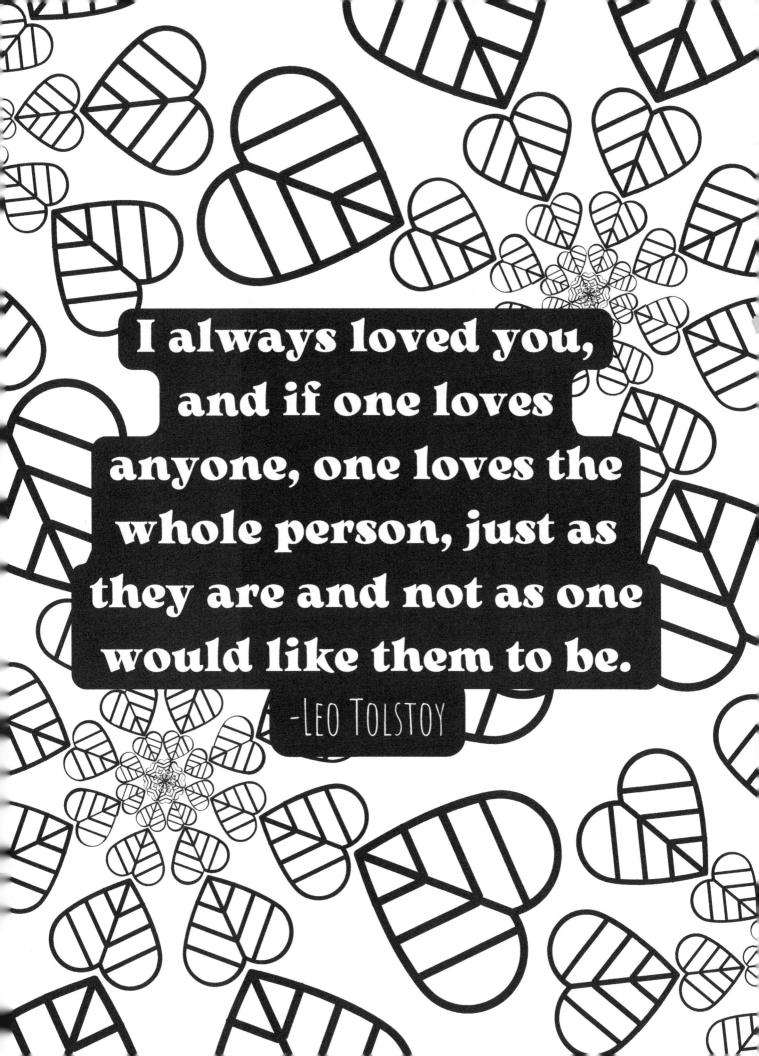

I always loved you, and if one loves anyone, one loves the whole person, just as they are and not as one would like them to be.

-Leo Tolstoy

ALL THE VARIETY, ALL THE CHARM, ALL THE BEAUTY OF LIFE IS MADE UP OF LIGHT AND SHADOW.

-Leo Tolstoy

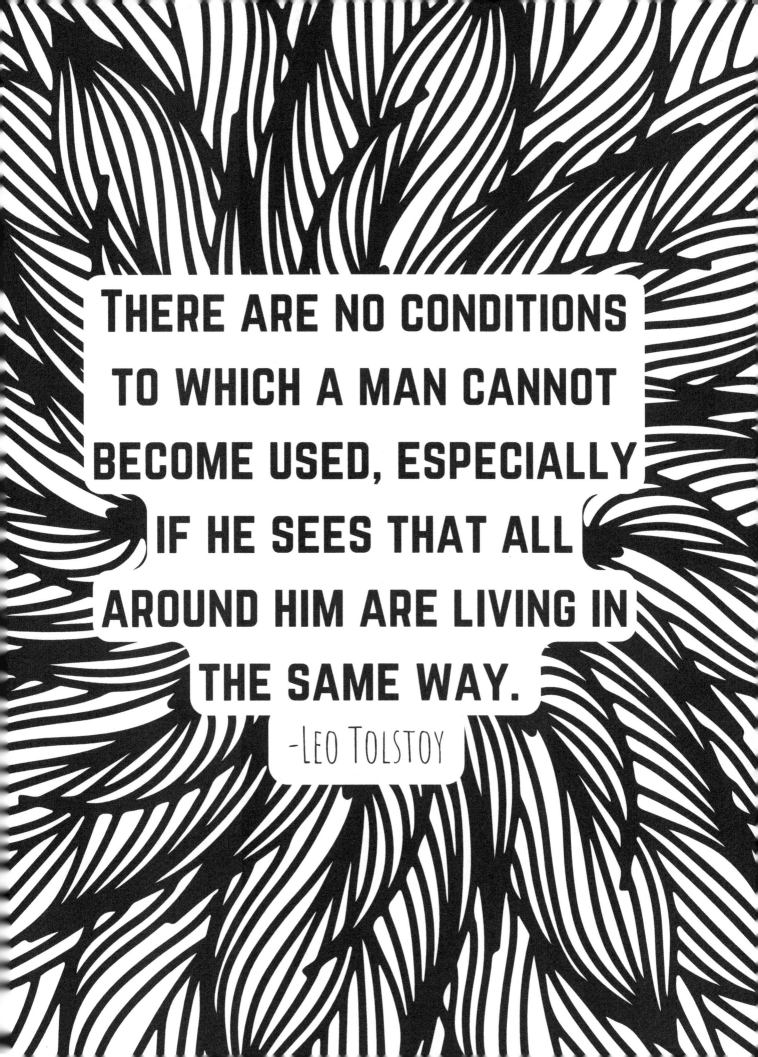

THERE ARE NO CONDITIONS TO WHICH A MAN CANNOT BECOME USED, ESPECIALLY IF HE SEES THAT ALL AROUND HIM ARE LIVING IN THE SAME WAY.

-LEO TOLSTOY

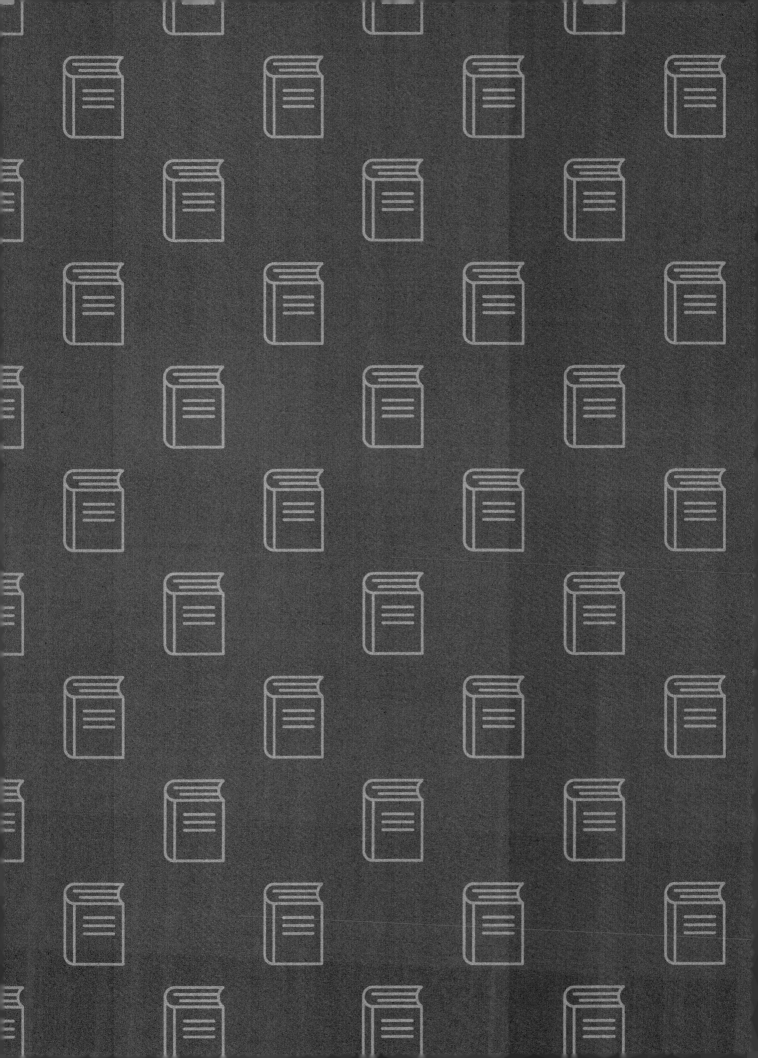

HE LOOKED AT HER AS A MAN LOOKS
AT A FADED FLOWER HE HAS
GATHERED, WITH DIFFICULTY
RECOGNIZING IN IT THE BEAUTY FOR
WHICH HE PICKED AND RUINED IT.

-LEO TOLSTOY

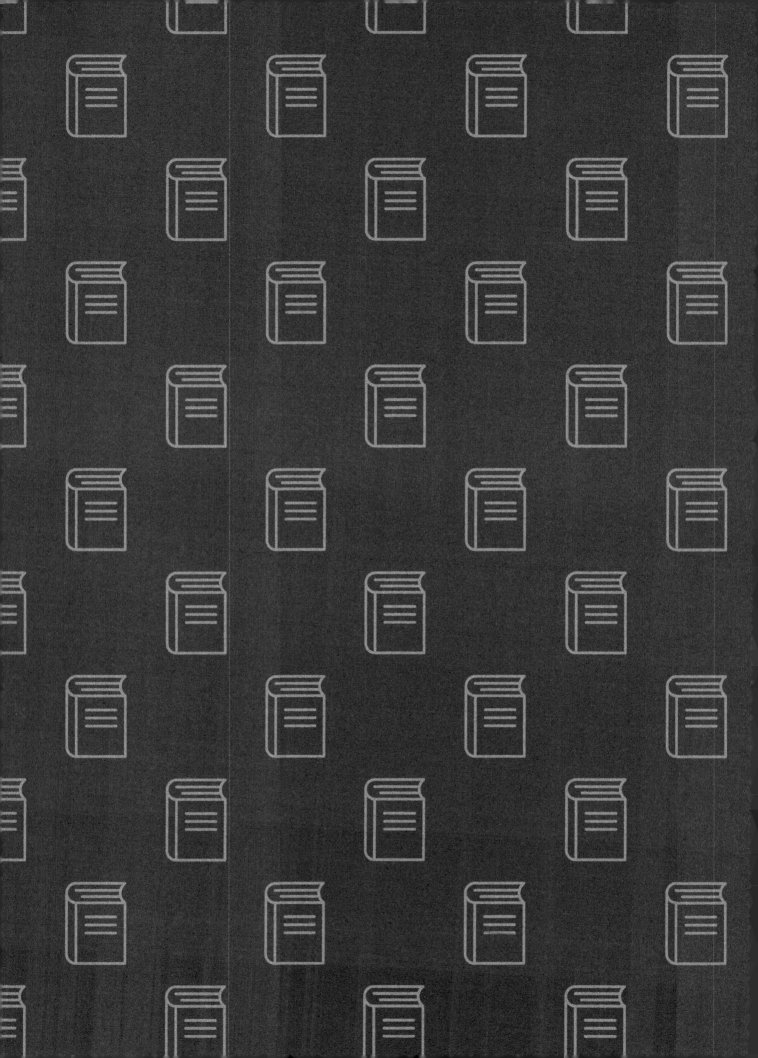

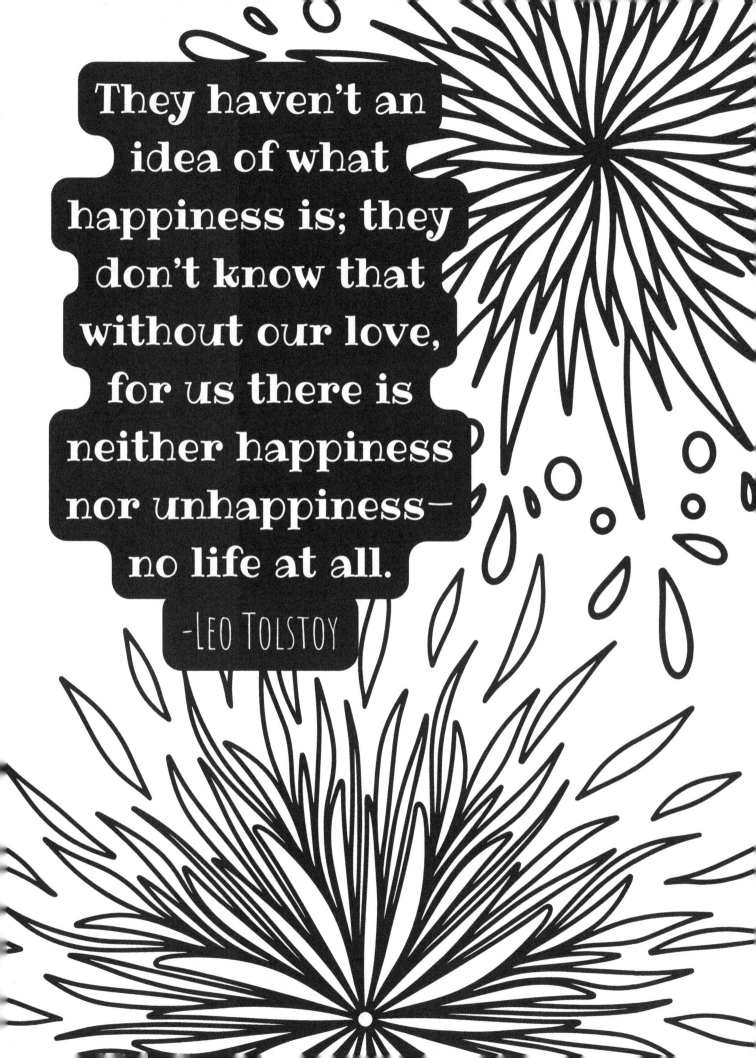

They haven't an idea of what happiness is; they don't know that without our love, for us there is neither happiness nor unhappiness— no life at all.

-Leo Tolstoy

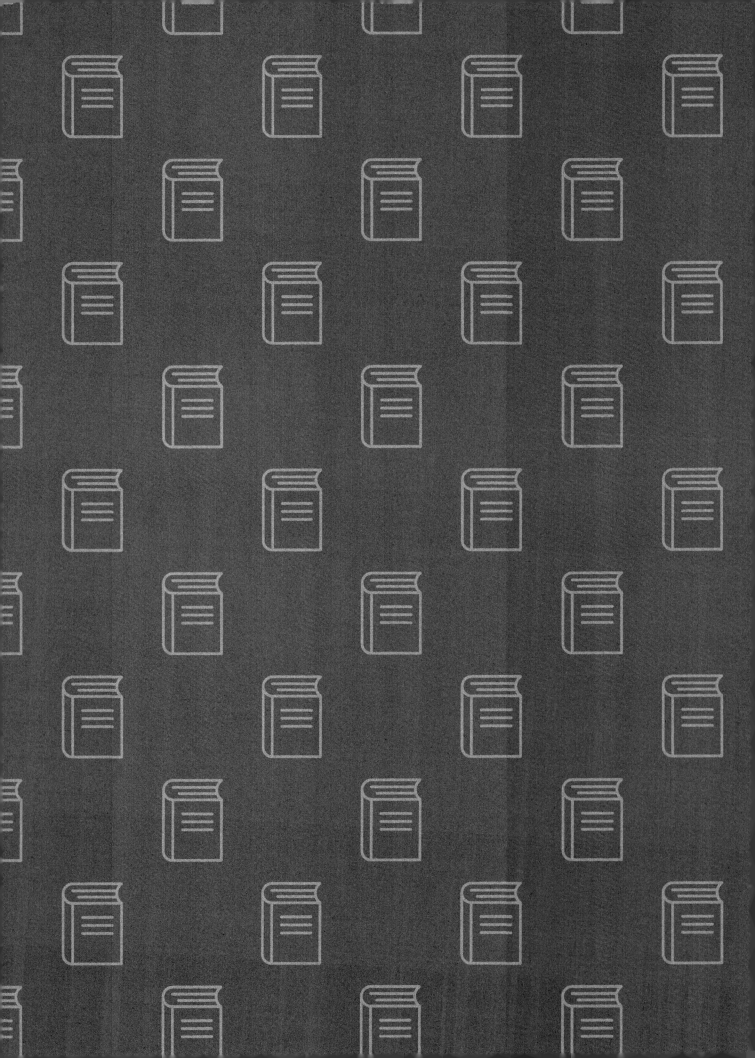

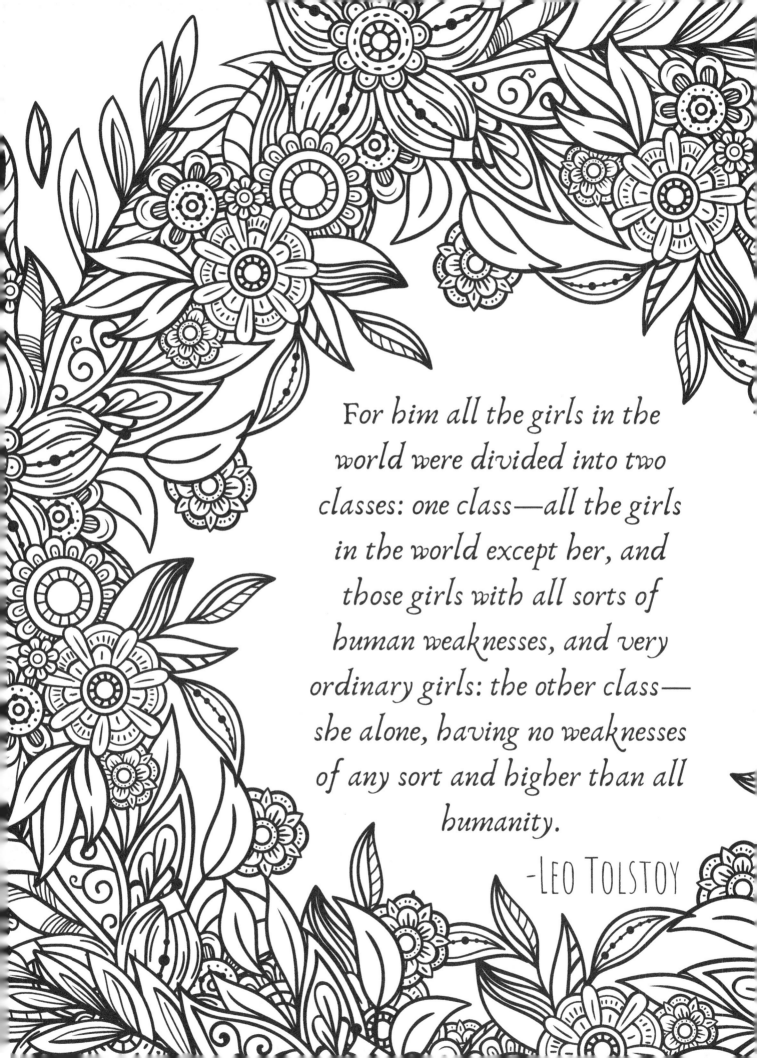

For him all the girls in the world were divided into two classes: one class—all the girls in the world except her, and those girls with all sorts of human weaknesses, and very ordinary girls: the other class— she alone, having no weaknesses of any sort and higher than all humanity.

-Leo Tolstoy

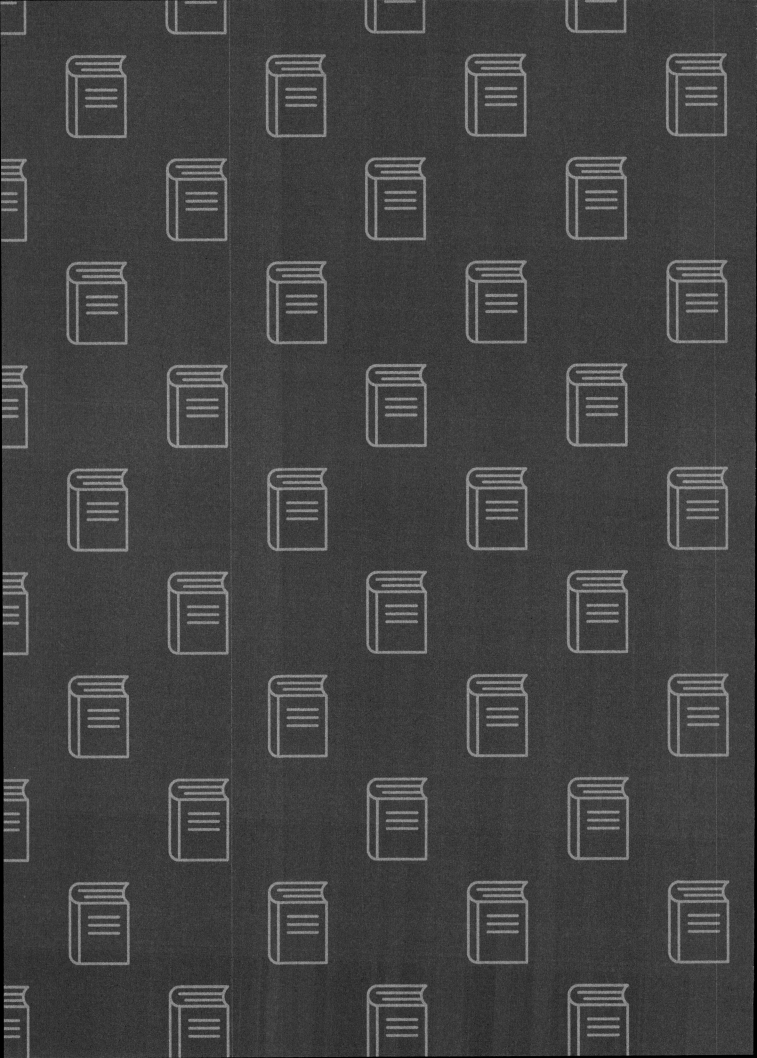

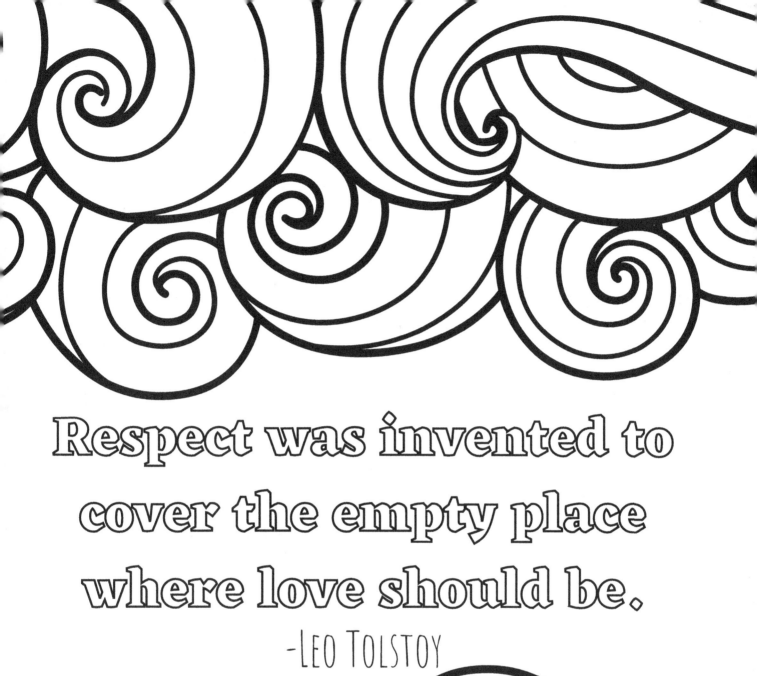

Respect was invented to cover the empty place where love should be.

-Leo Tolstoy

He knew she was there by the rapture and the terror that seized on his heart...she was as easy to find in that crowd as a rose among nettles. Everything was made bright by her. She was the smile that shed light on all round her.

-Leo Tolstoy

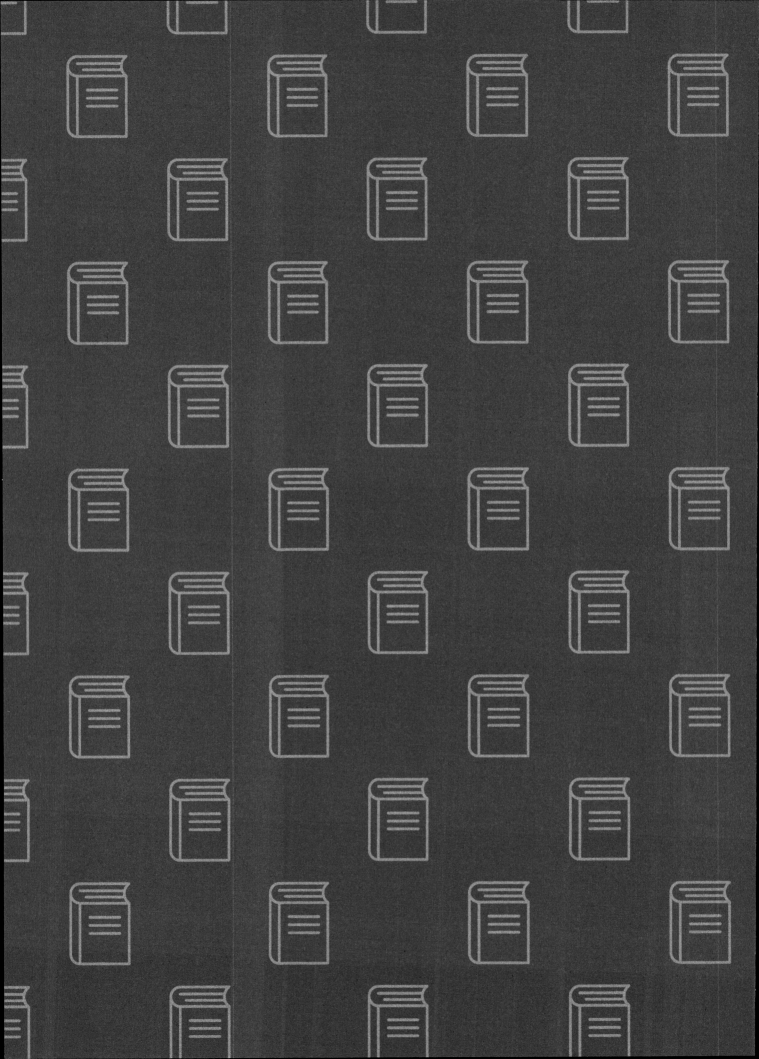

He walked down, for a long while avoiding looking at her as at the sun, but seeing her, as one does the sun, without looking.

-Leo Tolstoy

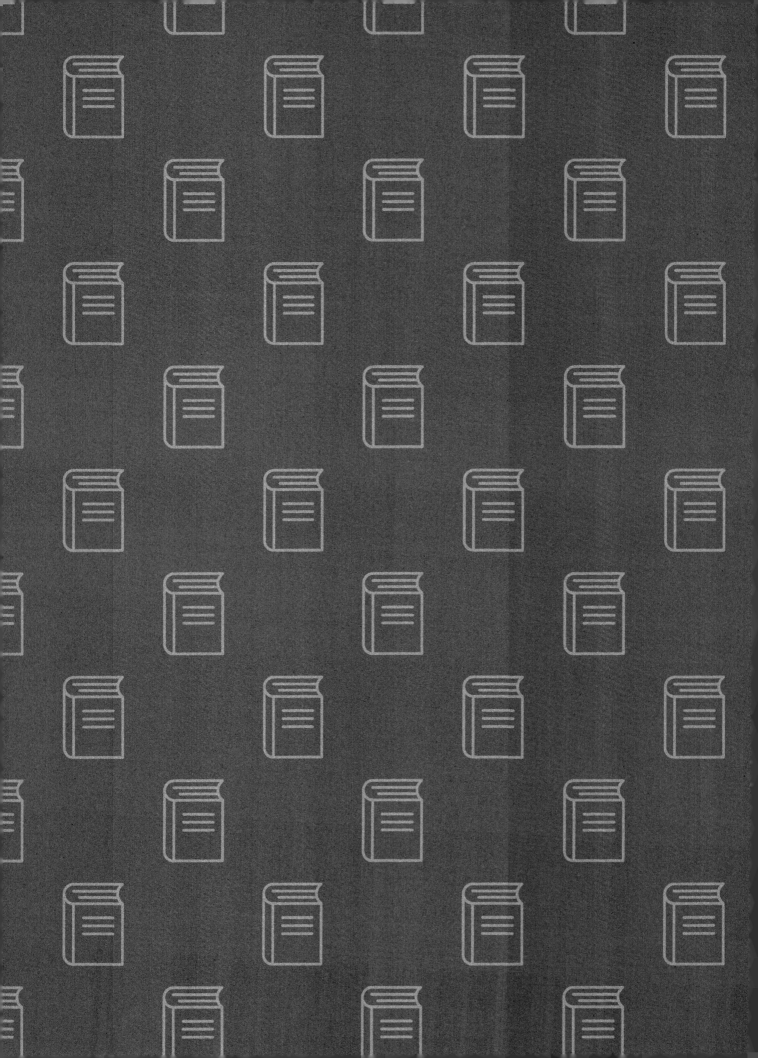

Ferreting in one's soul, one often ferrets out something that might have lain there unnoticed.

-Leo Tolstoy

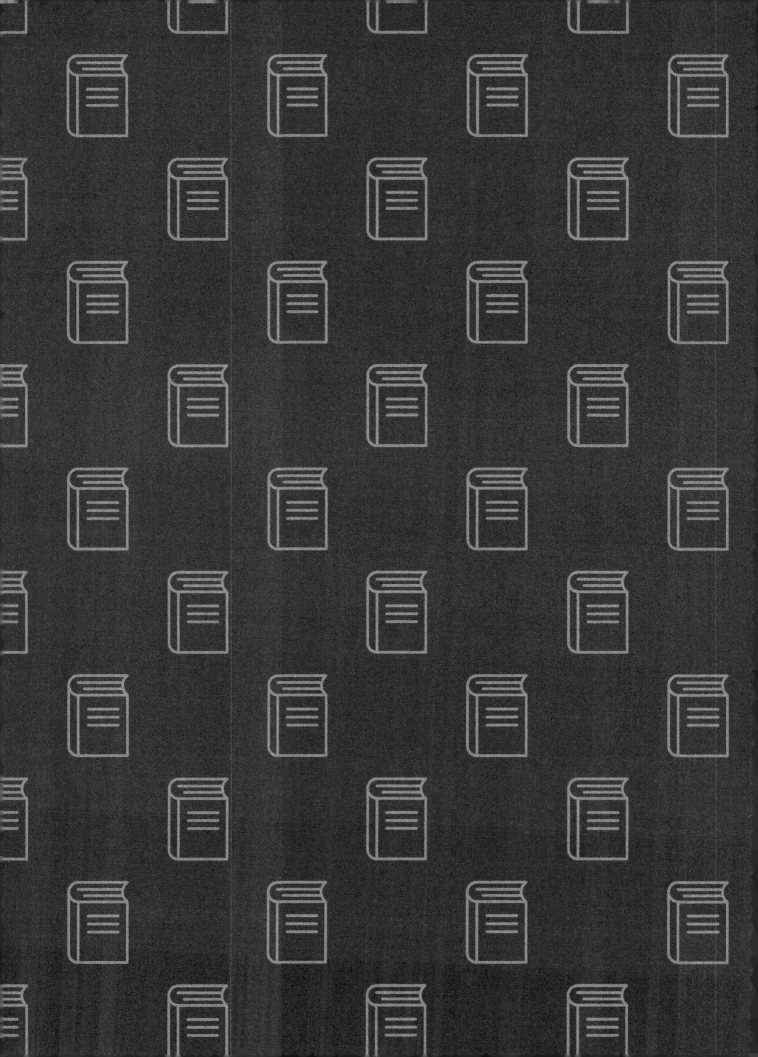

Anything's better than lying and deceit.

-Leo Tolstoy

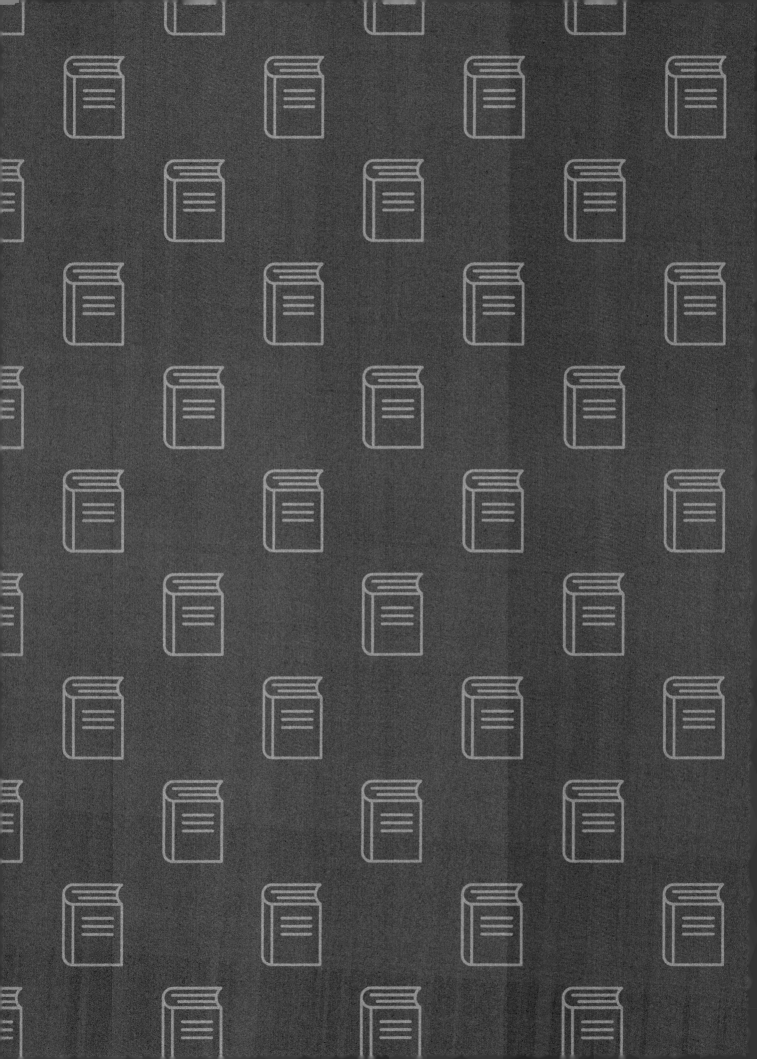

He soon felt that the realization of his desires gave him no more than a grain of sand out of the mountain of happiness he had expected. It showed him the mistake men make in picturing to themselves happiness as the realization of their desires.

-Leo Tolstoy

SOMETHING MAGICAL HAS HAPPENED TO ME, LIKE A DREAM, WHEN YOU'RE FRIGHTENED, PANIC-STRICKEN, AND ALL OF A SUDDEN YOU WAKE UP AND ALL THE HORRORS ARE NO MORE. I HAVE WAKED UP.

-LEO TOLSTOY

WHATEVER OUR DESTINY IS OR MAY BE, WE HAVE MADE IT OURSELVES, AND WE DO NOT COMPLAIN OF IT.

-LEO TOLSTOY

EVERY HEART HAS its OWN SKELEtONS.

-LEO TOLSTOY

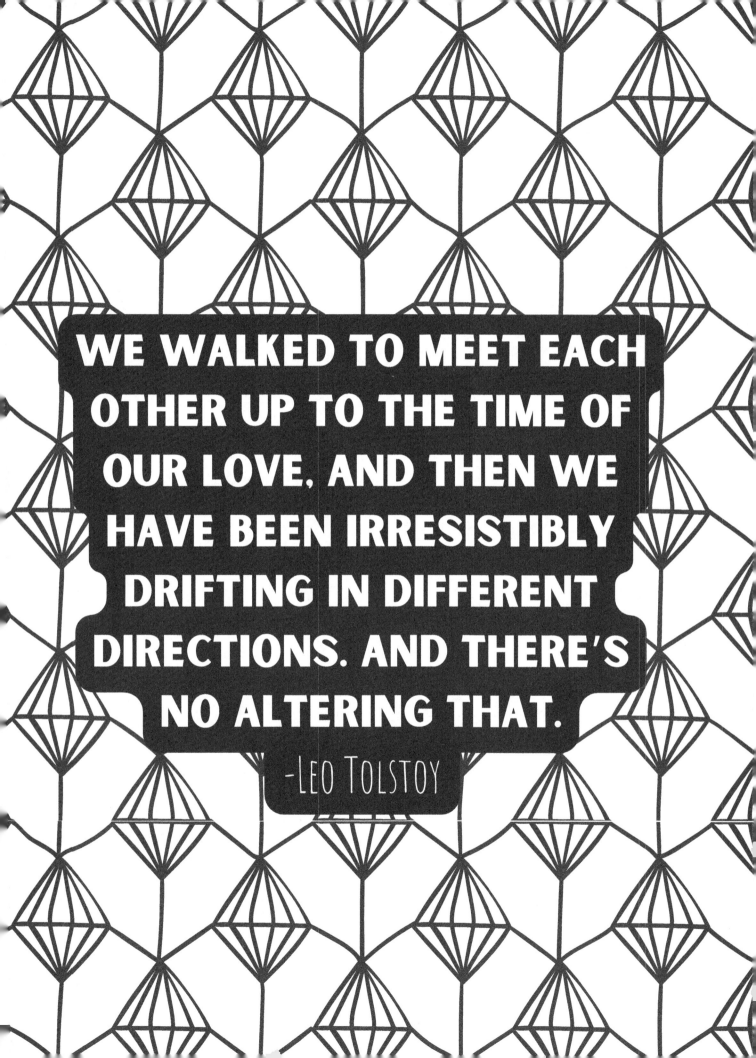

WE WALKED TO MEET EACH OTHER UP TO THE TIME OF OUR LOVE, AND THEN WE HAVE BEEN IRRESISTIBLY DRIFTING IN DIFFERENT DIRECTIONS. AND THERE'S NO ALTERING THAT.

-Leo Tolstoy

Not one word, not one gesture of yours shall I, could I, ever forget.
-LEO TOLSTOY

ENOUGH OR NOT ENOUGH, WE MUST MAKE IT DO.

-LEO TOLSTOY

SHE SMILED AT HIM, AND AT HER OWN FEARS.

-LEO TOLSTOY

Don't all the theories of philosophy do the same, trying by the path of thought, which is strange and not natural to man, to bring him to a knowledge of what he has known long ago, and knows so certainly that he could not live at all without it?

-Leo Tolstoy

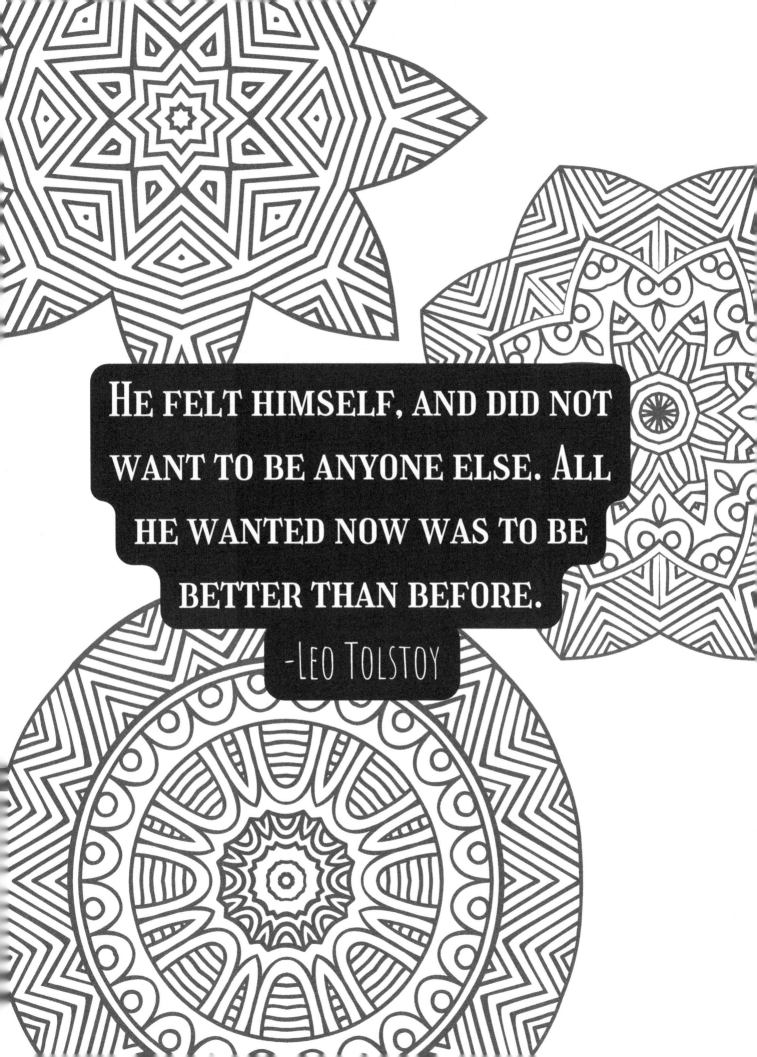

HE FELT HIMSELF, AND DID NOT WANT TO BE ANYONE ELSE. ALL HE WANTED NOW WAS TO BE BETTER THAN BEFORE.

-LEO TOLSTOY

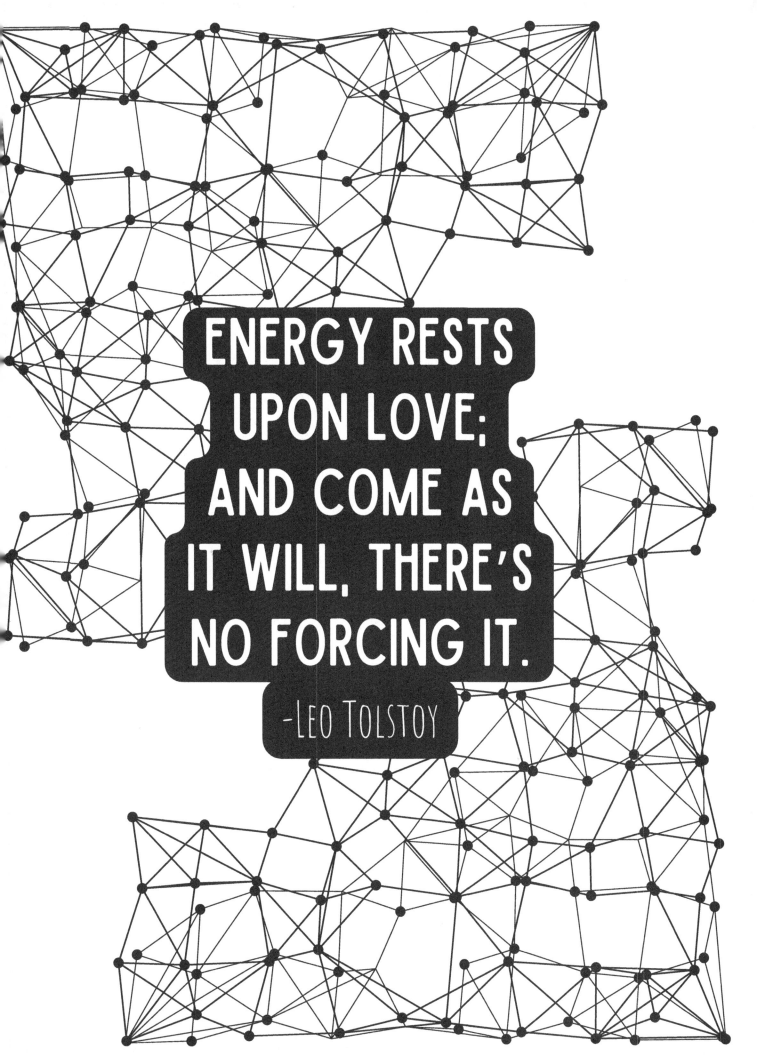

ENERGY RESTS UPON LOVE; AND COME AS IT WILL, THERE'S NO FORCING IT.

-Leo Tolstoy

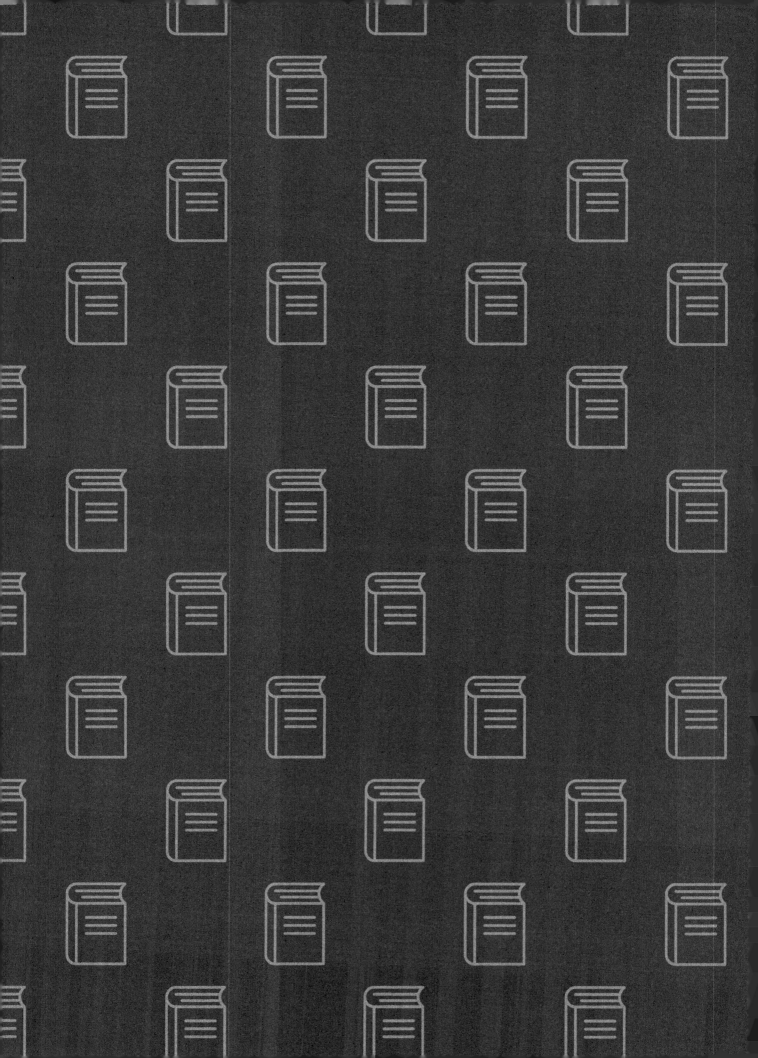

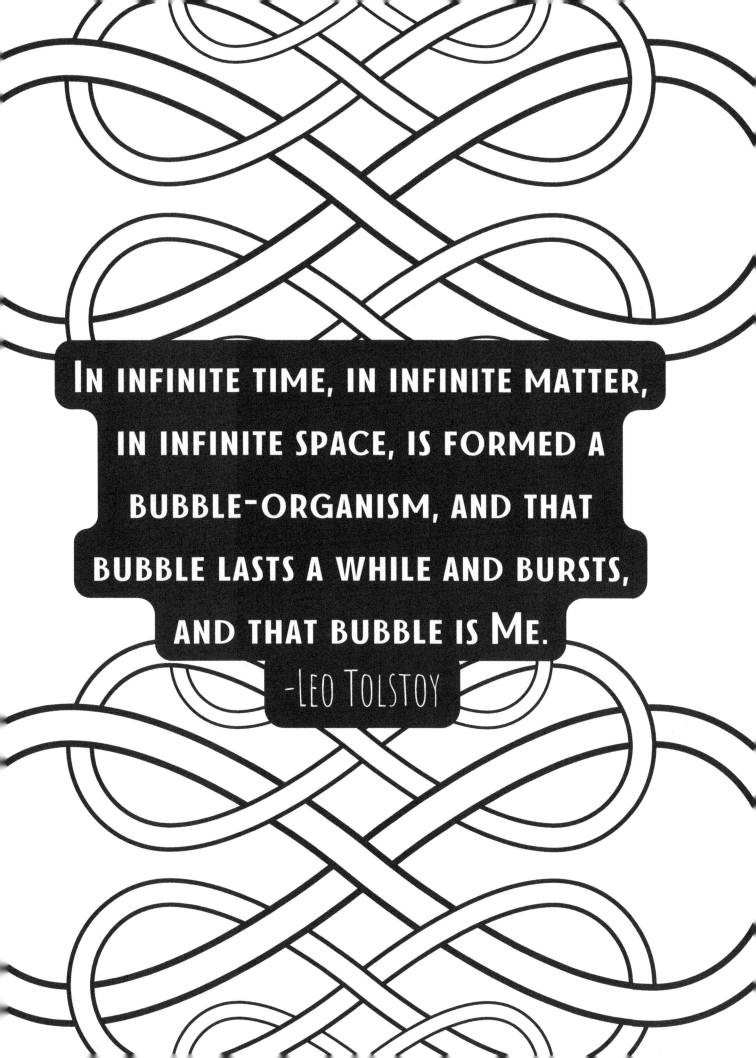

In infinite time, in infinite matter, in infinite space, is formed a bubble-organism, and that bubble lasts a while and bursts, and that bubble is Me.

-Leo Tolstoy

WHERE LOVE ENDS, HATE BEGINS.

-LEO TOLSTOY

ALL THIS WORLD OF OURS IS NOTHING BUT A SPECK OF MILDEW, WHICH HAS GROWN UP ON A TINY PLANET. AND FOR US TO SUPPOSE WE CAN HAVE SOMETHING GREAT—IDEAS, WORK—IT'S ALL DUST AND ASHES.

—Leo Tolstoy

WHAT DO THEY WANT TO
ARGUE FOR? NO ONE EVER
CONVINCES ANYONE.
-Leo Tolstoy

What's so awful is that one can't tear up the past by its roots.

-Leo Tolstoy

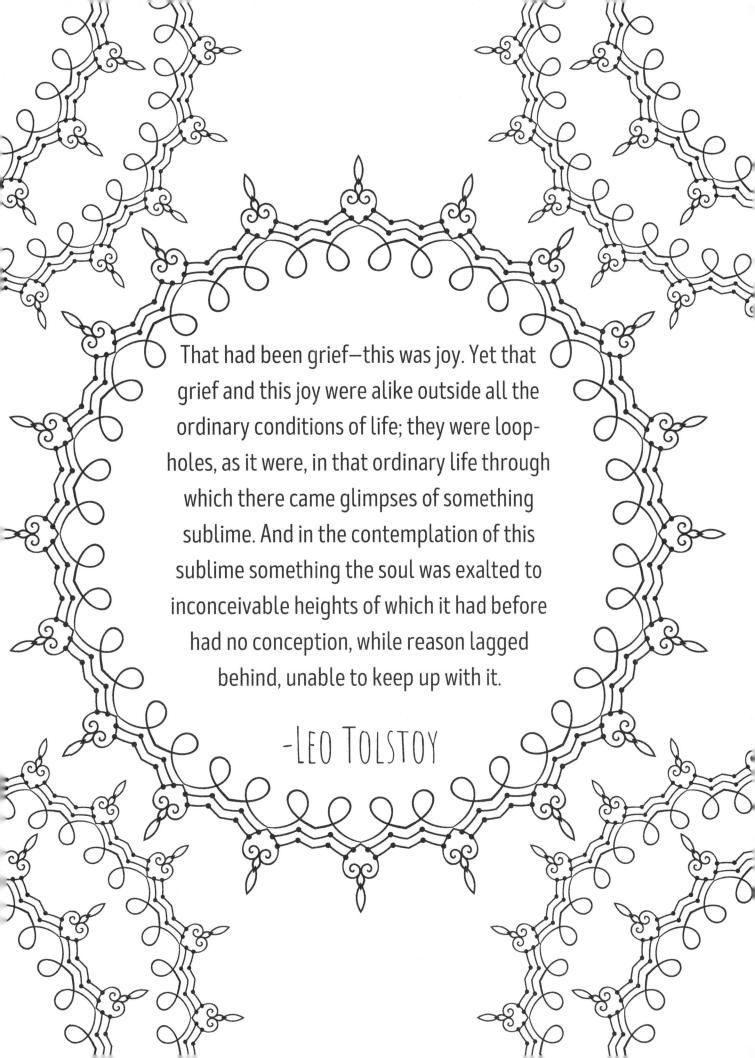

That had been grief—this was joy. Yet that grief and this joy were alike outside all the ordinary conditions of life; they were loopholes, as it were, in that ordinary life through which there came glimpses of something sublime. And in the contemplation of this sublime something the soul was exalted to inconceivable heights of which it had before had no conception, while reason lagged behind, unable to keep up with it.

-Leo Tolstoy

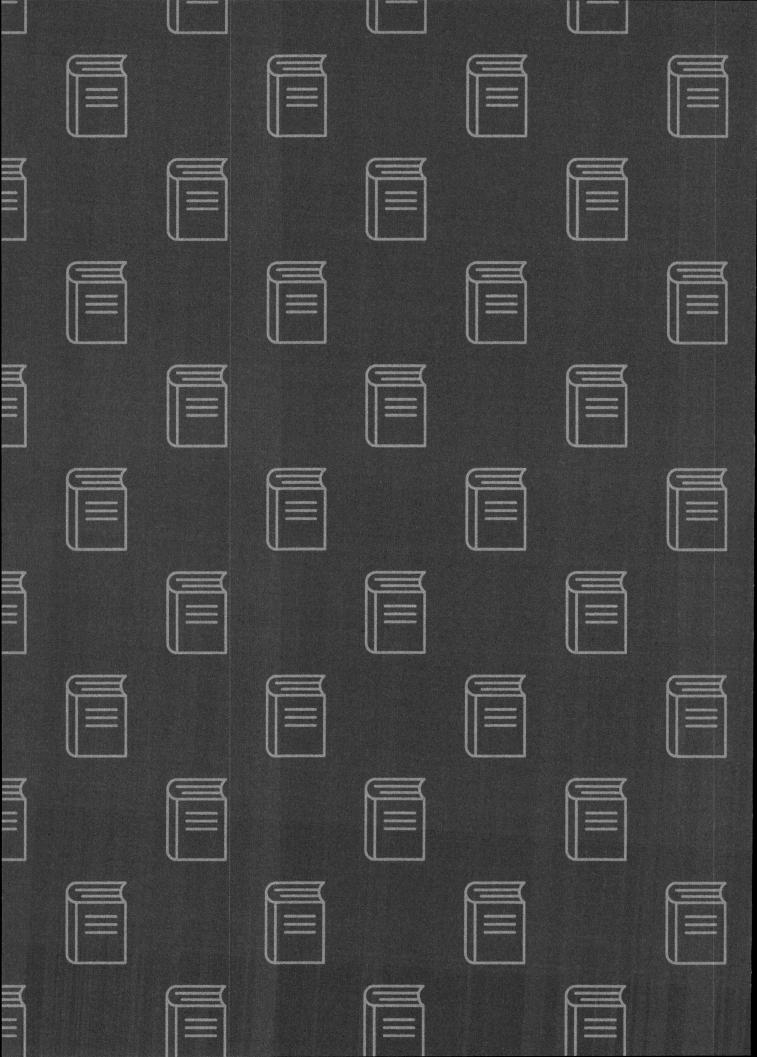

IF YOU LOOK FOR PERFECTION, YOU WILL NEVER BE SATISFIED.

-LEO TOLSTOY

Spring is the time for plans and projects.

-Leo Tolstoy

Love, why I don't like the word is that it means too much to me, far more than you can understand.

—Leo Tolstoy

Enjoyment lies in the search for truth, not in the finding it.

-LEO TOLSTOY

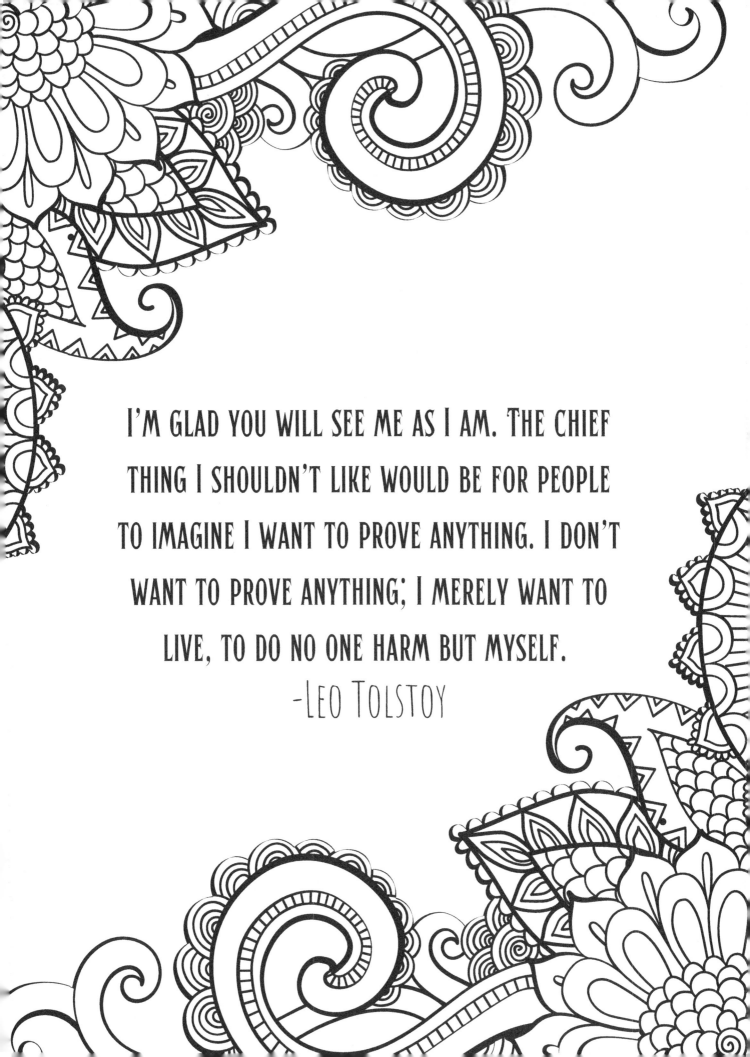

I'M GLAD YOU WILL SEE ME AS I AM. THE CHIEF THING I SHOULDN'T LIKE WOULD BE FOR PEOPLE TO IMAGINE I WANT TO PROVE ANYTHING. I DON'T WANT TO PROVE ANYTHING; I MERELY WANT TO LIVE, TO DO NO ONE HARM BUT MYSELF.
-Leo Tolstoy

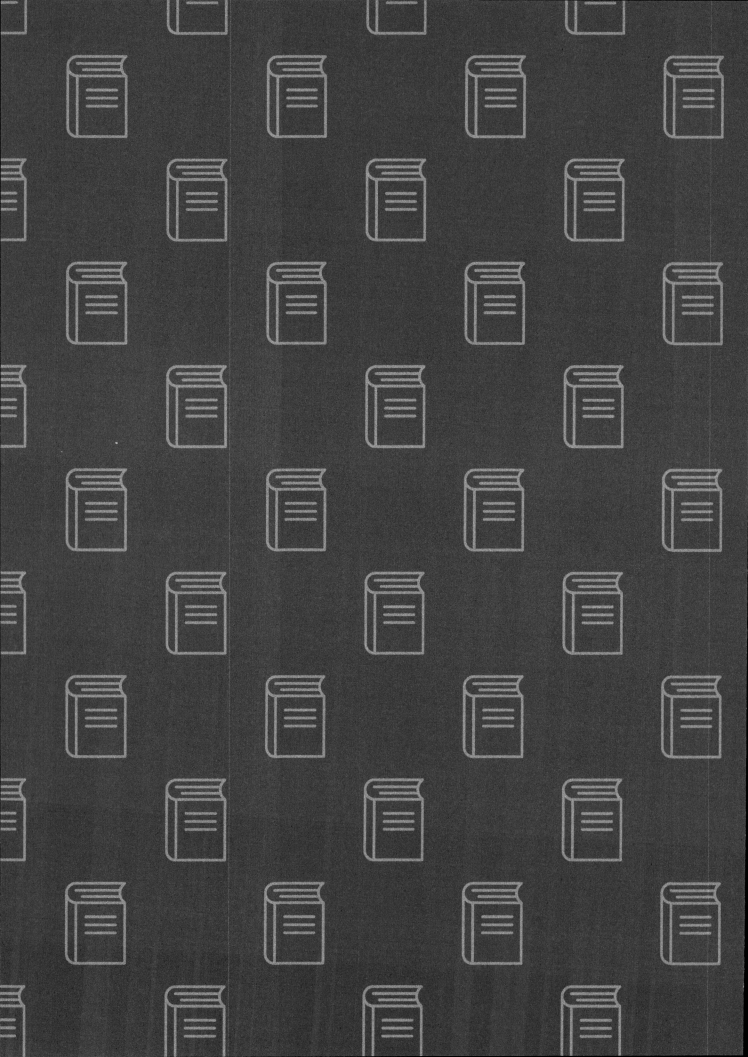

ONE HAS BUT TO FORGET
ONESELF AND LOVE OTHERS,
AND ONE WILL BE CALM,
HAPPY, AND NOBLE.

-Leo Tolstoy

Love those that hate you.

-LEO TOLSTOY

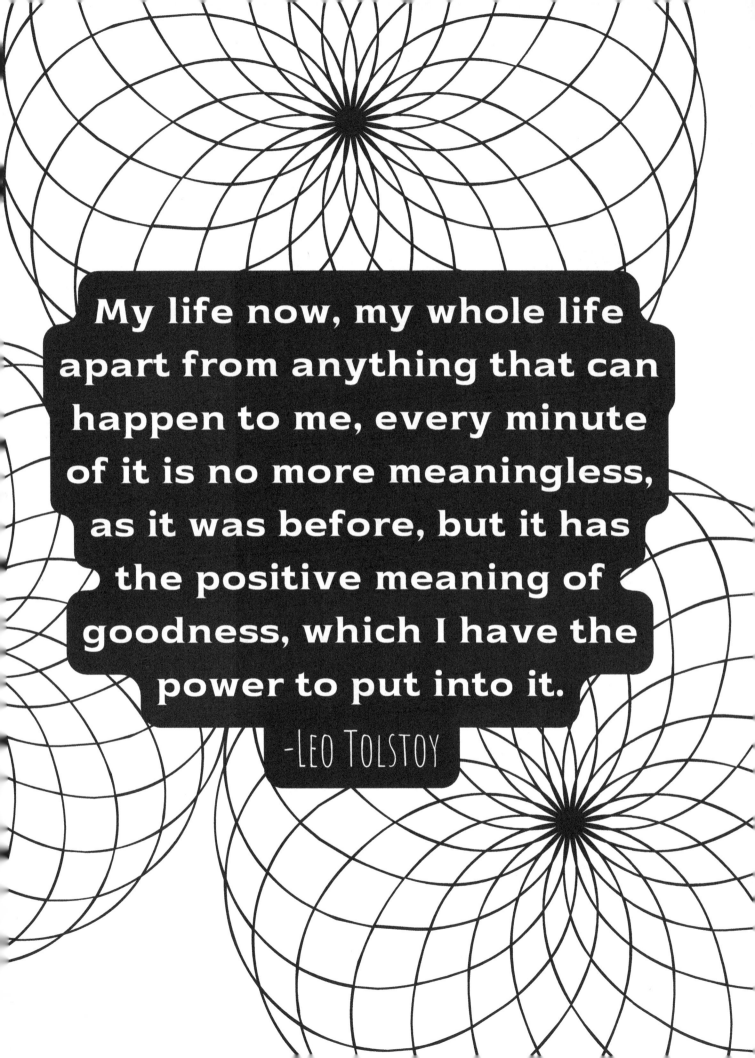

My life now, my whole life apart from anything that can happen to me, every minute of it is no more meaningless, as it was before, but it has the positive meaning of goodness, which I have the power to put into it.

-Leo Tolstoy

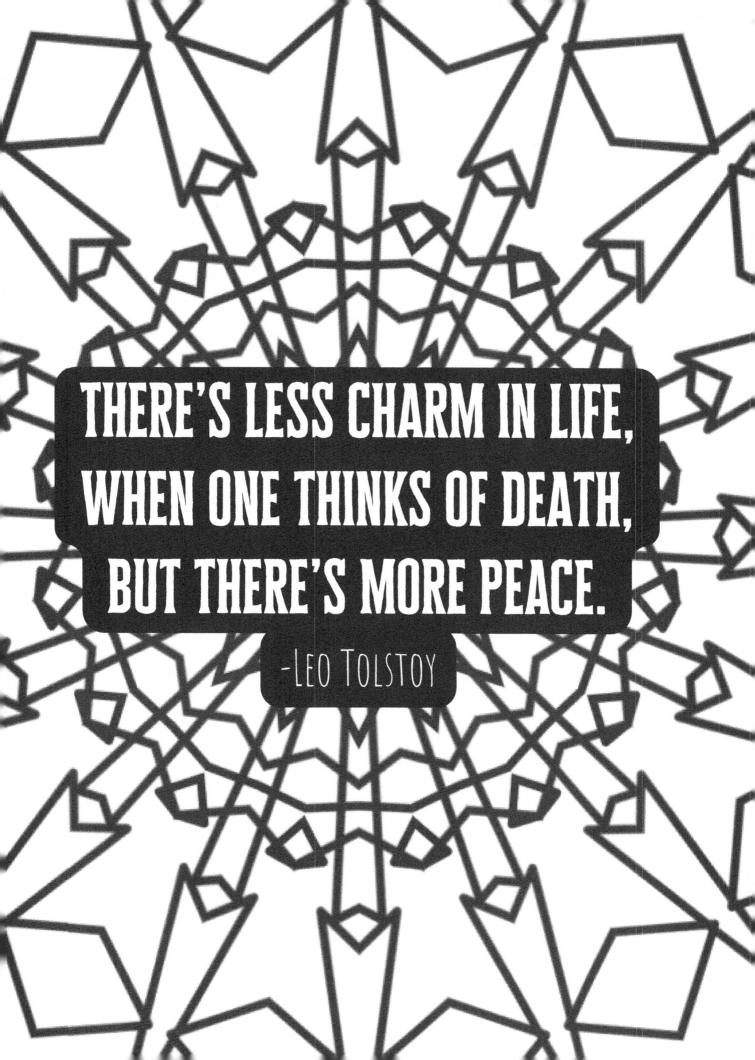

THERE'S LESS CHARM IN LIFE, WHEN ONE THINKS OF DEATH, BUT THERE'S MORE PEACE.

-Leo Tolstoy

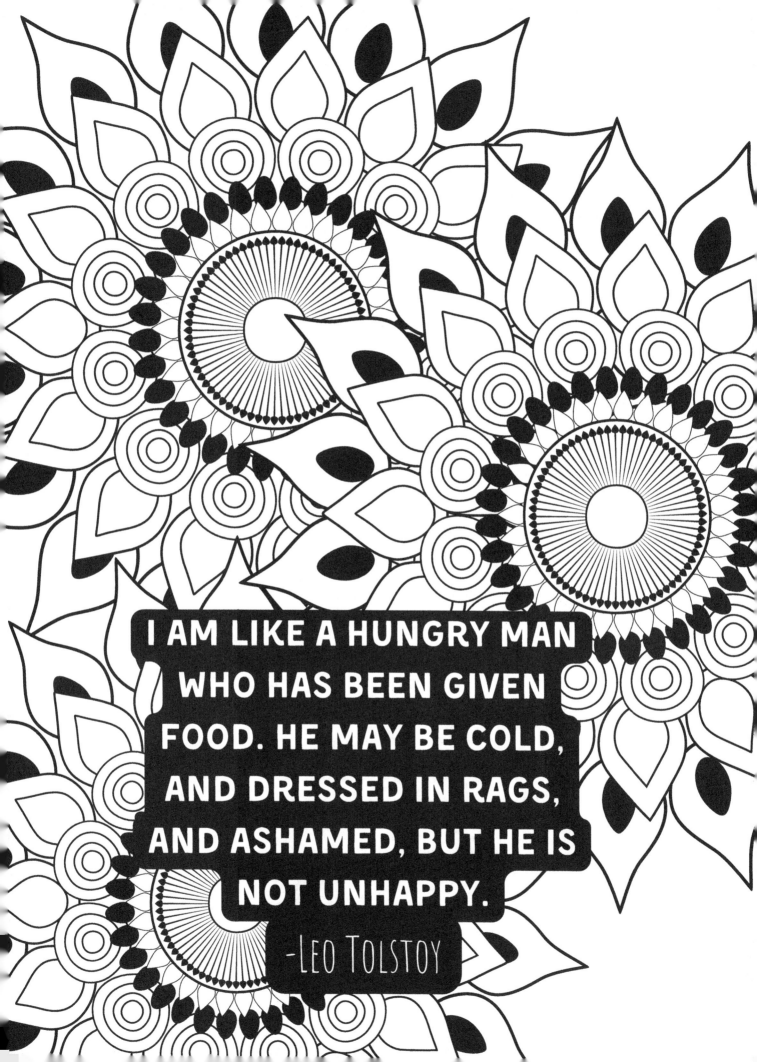

I AM LIKE A HUNGRY MAN WHO HAS BEEN GIVEN FOOD. HE MAY BE COLD, AND DRESSED IN RAGS, AND ASHAMED, BUT HE IS NOT UNHAPPY.

-LEO TOLSTOY

He could not be mistaken. There were no other eyes like those in the world. There was only one creature in the world that could concentrate for him all the brightness and meaning of life. It was she.

-Leo Tolstoy

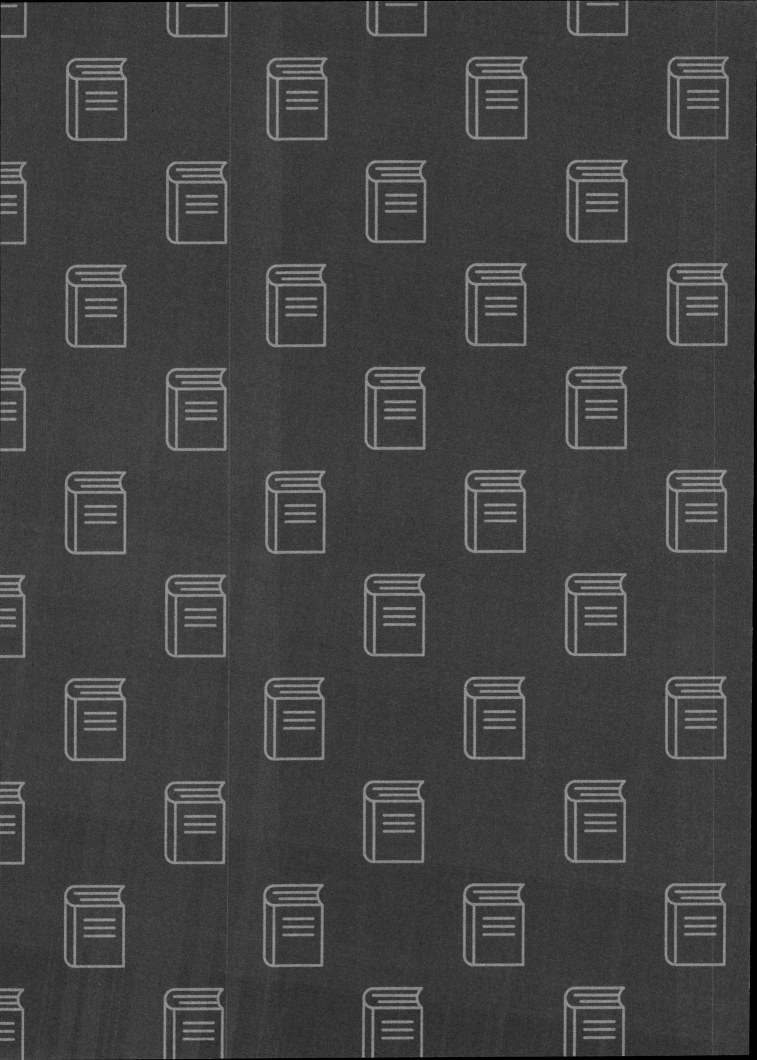

What always struck him in her as something unlooked for, was the expression of her eyes, soft, serene, and truthful, and above all, her smile, which always transported Levin to an enchanted world, where he felt himself softened and tender, as he remembered himself in some days of his early childhood.

-Leo Tolstoy

The more he did nothing, the less time he had to do anything.

-Leo Tolstoy

How much that seemed to me then splendid and out of reach has become worthless, while what I had then has gone out of my reach forever!

-Leo Tolstoy

It's hard to love a woman and do anything.

-LEO TOLSTOY

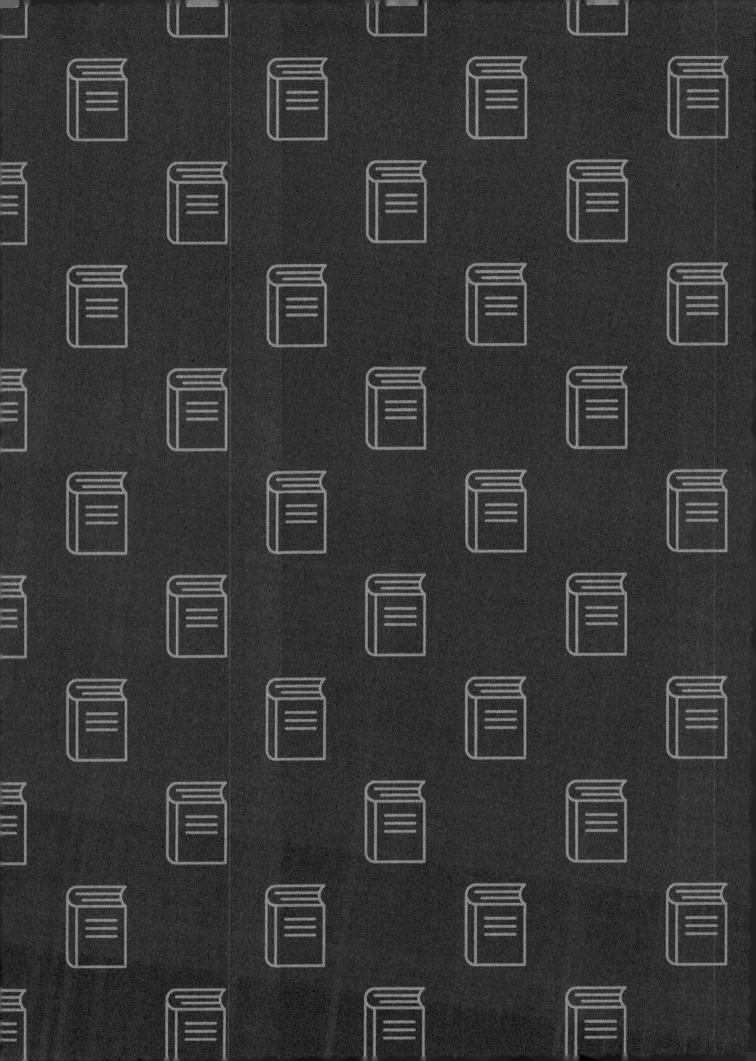

THERE WAS NO SOLUTION, BUT THAT UNIVERSAL SOLUTION WHICH LIFE GIVES TO ALL QUESTIONS, EVEN THE MOST COMPLEX AND INSOLUBLE. THAT ANSWER IS: ONE MUST LIVE IN THE NEEDS OF THE DAY—THAT IS, FORGET ONESELF.

-LEO TOLSTOY

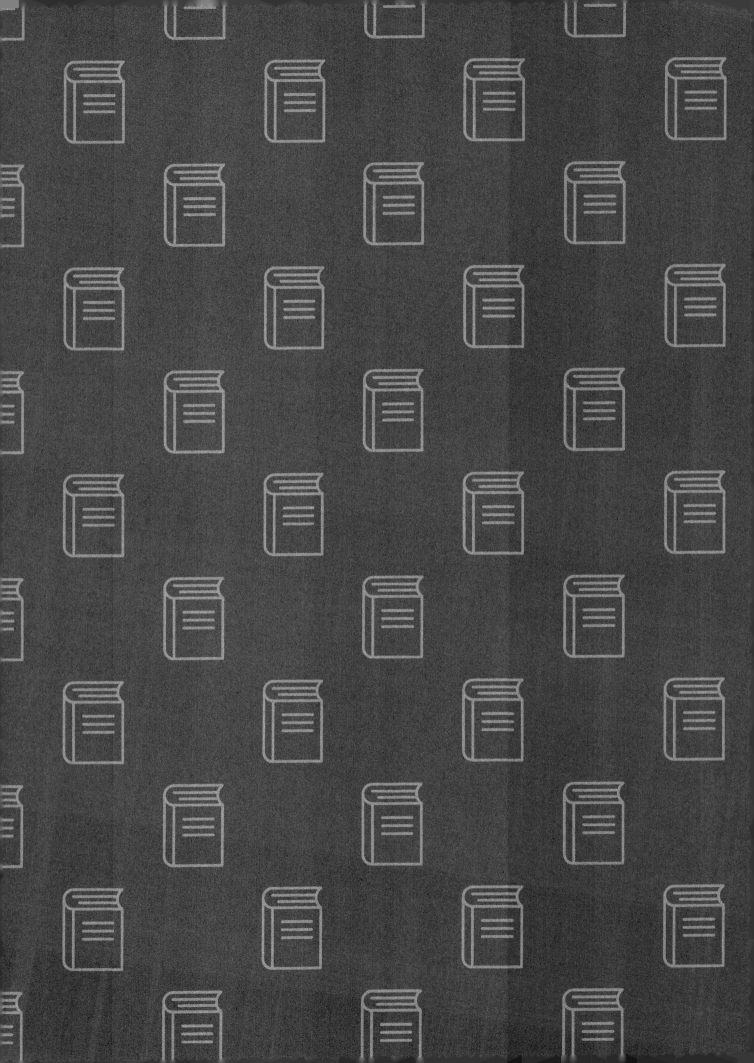

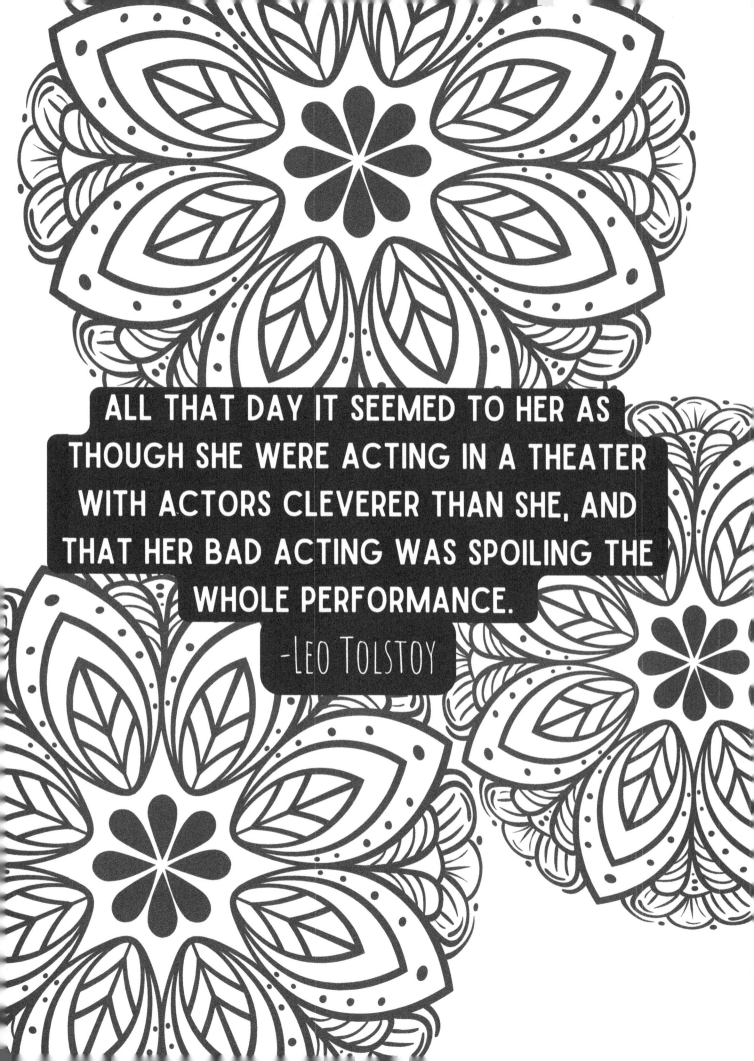

ALL THAT DAY IT SEEMED TO HER AS THOUGH SHE WERE ACTING IN A THEATER WITH ACTORS CLEVERER THAN SHE, AND THAT HER BAD ACTING WAS SPOILING THE WHOLE PERFORMANCE.

-LEO TOLSTOY

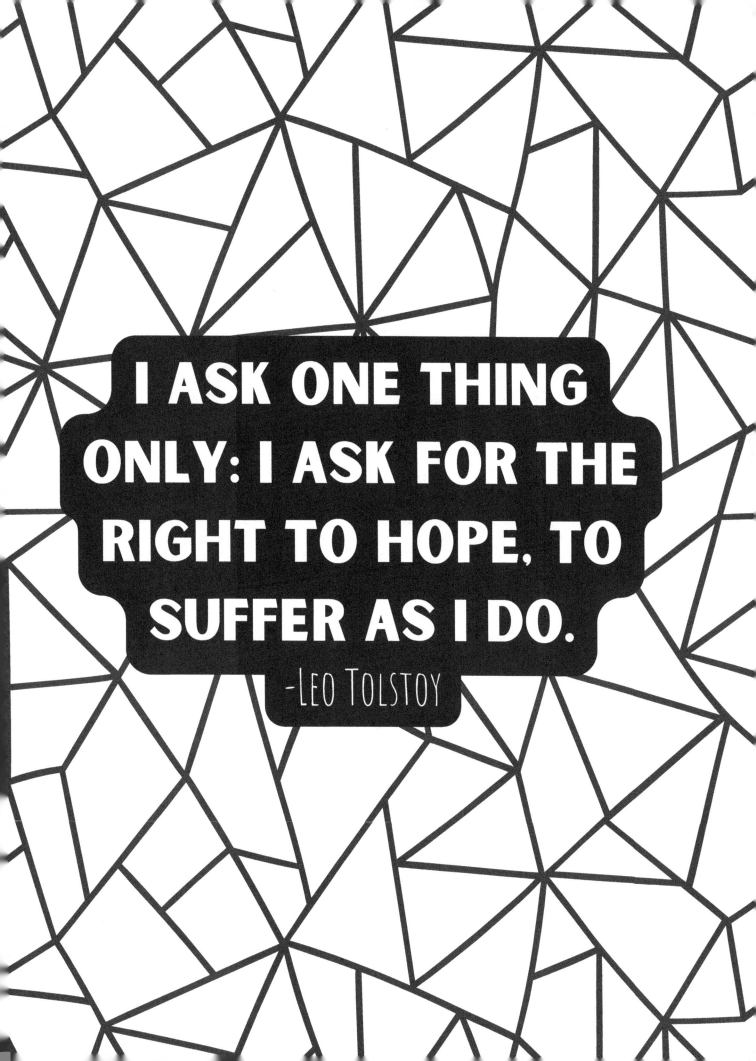

I ASK ONE THING ONLY: I ASK FOR THE RIGHT TO HOPE, TO SUFFER AS I DO.

-Leo Tolstoy

DON'T YOU KNOW THAT YOU'RE ALL MY LIFE TO ME? BUT I KNOW NO PEACE, AND I CAN'T GIVE IT TO YOU; ALL MYSELF—AND LOVE ... YES. I CAN'T THINK OF YOU AND MYSELF APART. YOU AND I ARE ONE TO ME. AND I SEE NO CHANCE BEFORE US OF PEACE FOR ME OR FOR YOU. I SEE A CHANCE OF DESPAIR, OF WRETCHEDNESS ... OR I SEE A CHANCE OF BLISS.

-LEO TOLSTOY

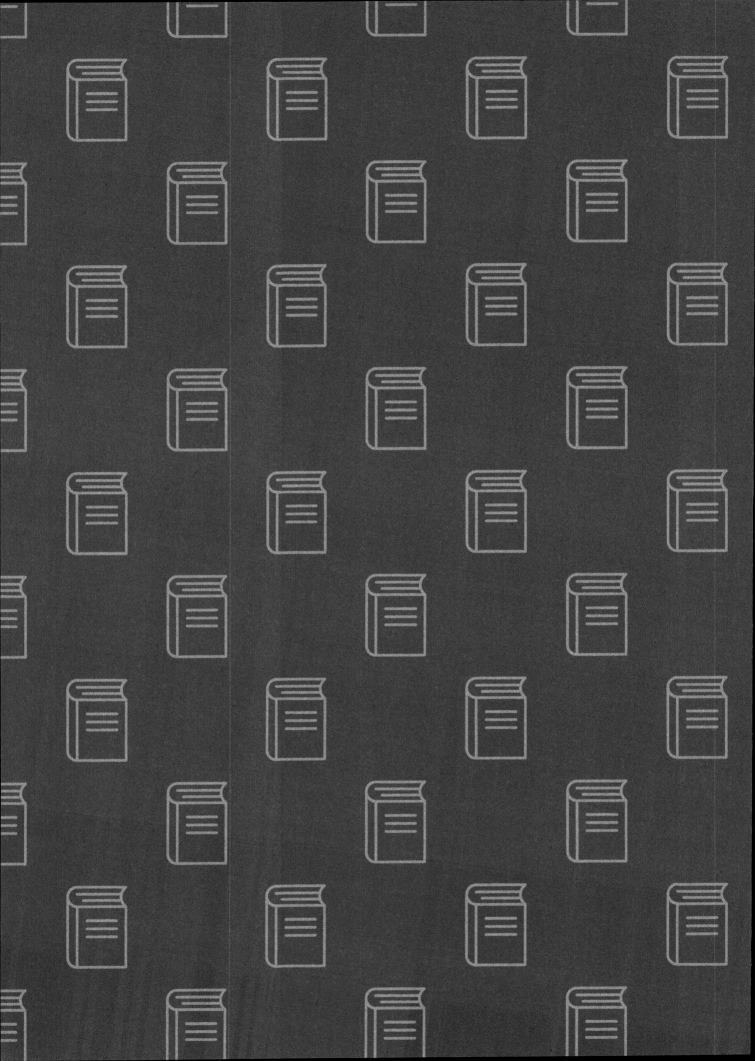

By reason could I have arrived at knowing that I must love my neighbor and not oppress him? I was told that in my childhood, and I believed it gladly, for they told me what was already in my soul. But who discovered it? Not reason. Reason discovered the struggle for existence, and the law that requires us to oppress all who hinder the satisfaction of our desires. That is the deduction of reason. But loving one's neighbor reason could never discover, because it's irrational.

-Leo Tolstoy

Made in the USA
Las Vegas, NV
16 December 2024

14462103R00057